THE AUTHOR Roger Tagholm ('Straphanger') was born in 1957 in Croydon and then moved to LA. Unfortunately, LA stands for Lower
Addiscombe which is also in Croydon. A journalist for nearly ten years,
he has written for a wide range of publications including the *Guardian*,
Punch and *Time Out*. He is currently on the staff of *Publishing News*, has
a weekly column in *Nine to Five*, London's 'commuter' magazine, and
lives with his wife and two children in Wimbledon, at the end of the
District and Northern Lines.

NOT

Poems/on the Underground

A parody
edited by
'Straphanger'

ROGER TAGHOLM

FIFTH EDITION

First four cancelled due to an earlier incident at Cockfosters

THE WINDRUSH PRESS

First published in Great Britain in 1996
by The Windrush Press, in association with Cassell & Co.
Morton-in-Marsh,
Gloucestershire

Cassell & Co.
Wellington House
125 Strand, London WC2R 0BB

Reprinted in 1997, 1999, 2001

British Library Cataloguing in Publication Data
A catalogue record for this book is available from the British Library

ISBN 0 900075 99 6

Typeset by Archetype, Condicote, Cheltenham
Printed and bound in Great Britain by Biddles Ltd, *www.biddles.co.uk*

DEDICATION

For my parents, who know most of the originals,
and for Billy Barnaby Tagholm,
born on 10th November 1995. Not forgetting
Ann – thanks for the straphangers.

In the beginning . . .

In the beginning God created the
Heaven and the earth and parts of the Northern.
And the earth was without form,
And void, like Colliers Wood;
And darkness was upon the face of the deep,
Particularly at Hampstead where it was deepest of all;
And God said, 'Let there be light': and there was
Light (excepting the southbound platform at Tooting Bec
Which had suffered an earlier blow-out),
And God called the light Day, and the darkness he called
The Underground.

With apologies to the Bible
(St James's Park version)

CONTENTS

THE POEMS

Commuters of the world unite! You have nothing to lose but your Travelcards.

KARL MARX, Tottenham Court Road Station 1882.

This be the Verse
(to recite as you wait. And wait)

They fuck you up, the Northern Line trains,
They may not mean to, but they do.
They say they're coming through Camden
Whereas you know they're stuck at Waterloo.

But they were fucked up in their turn
By governments who didn't cough up the money,
Who half the time were unnecessarily stern
About buskers who were only trying to be funny.

Governments hand on misery to man.
It deepens like the Northern Line itself.
Get off the trains as early as you can
And don't commute at all if you want your health.

With apologies to PHILIP LARKIN

Hamlet at Kennington

Tube, or not Tube: that is the question:
Whether 'tis nobler in the mind to suffer
The stinks and elbows of obnoxious passengers,
Or to take refuge in your Walkman,
And by ignoring end them? To die: to nod off:
No more; and, by nodding off to say we end
The bone-ache, the delays, the thousand disturbances
The Underground is heir to, 'tis an escape
Devoutly to be wish'd. To die, to have a kip;
To sleep; perchance to miss our stop: ay, there's the rub.

With apologies to you know who

Composed upon Oxford Street

Earth has plenty to show more fair:
Dull would he be of soul who could enjoy
Sights so grating in their commerciality:
This Street now doth, like an old rag, defile
The beauty of the morning; noisy, full,
Shops, department stores, burger bars and boutiques lie
Open unto the pavement, and to the sky;
All tacky and glittering in the fume-fillled air.
Often did sun more beautifully bless
In his first splendour valley, rock or hill;
Ne'er saw I, and felt, a cacophany so deep!
The buses do charge at their own sweet will:
Dear God! the very pigeons seem tawdry and cheap;
And beneath the Street Londoners on the Central feel ill!

With apologies to WILLIAM WORDSWORTH

The Central and the Circle

The Central and the Circle,
When they are both full-known,
Of all the Lines that are on the Tube,
The Central bears the crown.

O the buttons of the doors,
And the running of the mice,
The litter on the grubby floors,
O Central Line so nice!

The Central bears a blossom,
At Tottenham Court Road,
Its name is Paolozzi,
Mad tiling à la mode!
O the buttons on the doors . . . .

The Central bears small end seats,
As soft as any lamb,
To sit on them as far as Ruislip,
Patience like the Son of Man!
O the buttons on the doors . . . .

The Central bears a strange loop,
From Wanstead to Woodford,
Riding on it through Grange Hill/Fairlop,
Will never make you bored!
O the buttons on the doors . . . .

The Central is so bright red,
Like roses in the park,
Of all the Lines that are in London,
The Central is the heart!
O the buttons on the doors . . . .

With apologies to carol singers everywhere

The Commuter

If I should die, think only this of me:
That there's some corner of a northbound platform
That is for ever late for work. There shall be
In that grubby concrete an even grubbier dust concealed;
A dust whom the office bore (Keith), bored, sent to sleep,
Gave, once, her photocopier to hate, her corridors to roam,
A body of the office's, bothered by office creeps,
Irritated by whip-rounds, always thankful to get home.

With apologies to RUPERT BROOKE

Jesus Addresses the Multitude
at Oxford Circus

Blessed are the Tube travellers; for they deserve the kingdom
of heaven.

Blessed are they that stand; for they shall be comforted
(eventually).

Blessed are the meek; for they shall inherit a seat (complete
with chewing gum),

Blessed are they who do hunger and thirst in the dark; for
them the platform Cadbury's machine is waiting (empty).

Blessed are the delayed; for they shall obtain mercy (one
day).

Blessed are the claustrophobics; for they shall see God down
there (standing too, no doubt).

Blessed are the ticket inspectors; for they shall be called the
sons of God (and a lot else besides).

Blessed are they who are prosecuted for righteousness' sake;
for theirs is the kingdom of heaven too – only heaven's in
Zone 12 (verses 5–7) and their ticket's for 3.

Blessed are ye, when men shall push you, and shove you,
and attempt all manner of falseness for a place on the
escalator.

Rejoice, and be exceedingly glad (or mad); for great is your
reward in heaven – that's if you get there;

unfortunately, as you've just heard, the next train terminates
at purgatory.

With apologies to Matthew 5: platforms 3–12

from **The Prologue to** *The Canterbury Tales*

Whan that Aprill with his shoures soote
The droghte of March hath perced to the roote,
And bathed the trains of Oakwood and Loughton
With tendre droppes of shoures all the way from Brighton
Aided by Zephirus (or was it Michael Fishe?)
Whose breath priketh every home and tree and satellite dishe,

Thanne do workers longen for to travel
To buye a ticket and let their problemes unravel.
Of where they go this booke shall be the tellynge
But first I must improve my spellynge!

With apologies to GEOFFREY CHAUCER

To His Coy Train Operator

Had we but world enough, and time,
This lateness, Driver, were no crime.
We would sit down and think which way
You could get us to Marble Arch
Before the end of the day.
But at my back I always hear
My employer's winged chariot (actually a
Ford Sierra) drawing near.
With P45 in hand he yells:
''Tis the second time this week!

You're out!'

And yonder before me lie
Deserts of vast eternity.

With apologies to ANDREW MARVELL

Anthem for Doomed Commuters

What passing-bells for these who travel as cattle?
Only the monotonous hiss of the rails.
Only the faltering announcers' inane prattle
Can mark out their hateful travails.
No memorials now for them; no prayers or buglemen,
Nor any voice of mourning save the whine, –
The tinny, wretched whine of many Walkmen;
And mobiles calling for them from sad offices down the line.

With apologies to WILFRED OWEN

from The Song of Hiawalthamstow

By the shores of Gitche Gumee,
Known too as the Lockwood Reservoir,
By the shining Banbury Big-Sea-Water
Near the great land of the Motorway-ways,
Not far from the hunters of Haringey,
With their Elders who worship Pee-cee
Stand the many red-brick wigwams of Hiawalthamstow.

Should you ask me, whence these stories?
Whence these legends and traditions,
With the odours of the High Street,
With the litter outside Dolcis,
With the rushing of great people
Who worship the Vic-tor-iah, God of All the Dark?
I should answer, I should tell you,
'From Epping Forest and Woodford Green,
From the Great Lakes off Snaresbrook Road,
From the land of the North Circular,
From the pavements of Wanstead,
From the chain stores, Pizza Huts and McDonald's
Where the young, the teenage squaws
Feed daily with no reason.'
I repeat them as I heard them,
From the lips of Sub-urb-iah
The God in whose arms we all dwell!

With apologies to HENRY WADSWORTH LONGFELLOW

Ozymandias, SE13

I met a traveller from an antique suburb
Who said: Two vast and trunkless legs of stone
Stand in Lewisham High Street . . . . Near them, outside M&S
Half sunk in the pavement, a shattered visage lies,
Whose frown and air of depression, tell that its sculptor
Well the cutbacks read. On a pedestal at its base
These words appear: 'My name is Margaret Moran, leader
of the council: Look on my works, ye Mighty, and Despair!'

With apologies to PERCY BYSSHE SHELLEY

What was on Larkin's Mind when he Wrote 'The Whitsun Weddings'

That Whitsun, I was late getting away:
A new delivery of porn had come in
And I was busy leafing through the
Bums and tits (lozenges of love!)
Before my train pulled out (as it were);
Then we were off, sliding down this
Phallic isle.

All that afternoon of heat we sped
South towards the Cross,
Past washing lines with lingerie faintly stained
And wives above kitchen sinks forlornly framed.
At first I didn't notice what a noise
The librarians made
Each station that we stopped at: British Rail coffee
Impedes perception of the world around us.
Yet once I focused I realized with a leap
That these duidecimal maidens would now my company keep.
To the library conference they were headed too
So I rang Kingers and said,
'Prepare a room for two. Larkin's about
And there could be leg-over too!'

With apologies to PHILIP LARKIN

Night Mail

This is the Night Mail crossing the county,
Bringing the cheque and all that bounty,

Letters for the rich, letters for the poor,
Cash for a gang, soon to run from the law.

Through the fields now, speeding with joy,
'Til Brucie gives a nod to Ronnie and the boys.

A sudden red light, the train lurches to a halt,
Men up the embankment! Faces stockinged, pulled taut!

The driver struggles, receives a cosh,
A bigger crime surely, than stealing the dosh.

To Leatherslade Farm the gang retreats,
To count its loot with a racing heartbeat.

Dawn arrives. Their raid is done.
Dew shines bright by the silent train,
While men peel away from a farm in the sun.

Years go by, some are caught, some die,
Johnny Rotten says he likes 'em, Phil Collins too.
Ronnie joins the Pistols and to Rio flies,

Publishers watch it all and lick their lips
Over lunch at the Groucho they forgive them their ills –
The Great Train Robbery means the ringing of tills.

So this was the Night Mail crossing the county,
Who is the greedier for chasing its bounty?

With apologies to W. H. AUDEN

Ode to Autumn, on the District

Region of twists and shallow routelessness,
Close bosom-friend of Putney Bridge;
Conspiring with him to trundle us south west
To take us across the Thames with no hint of umbrage;
Or through to Kew with little apology
(via Turnham Green, station of deepest ecology!);
On Ealing's fair(ish) Common the birds sing as of old,
While their trees shake their crests of russet and gold;
And all these gifts shall make true recompense
For the hours spent waiting on an Earl's Court bench
Through arrival after arrival that simply make no sense.

With apologies to JOHN KEATS

Chorleywood

Yes. I remember Chorleywood —
The name, because one afternoon
Of heat the Tube train blew up there
Magnificently. It was late June.

The brakes hissed. Someone keeled over.
No one left and no one came
On the bare platform. What I saw
Was Chorleywood – only the name

And adverts, advert-hoardings, and litter,
And litter bins, and newspapers dry,
Beyond all doubt as still and lonely fair
As the unconscious folk who on the floor did lie.

And for that minute a Tube mouse scurried
Close by, and round him, cheekier still,
All the Tube mice of Rickmansworth,
Pinner and the distant Northwood Hills

    With apologies to EDWARD THOMAS

Lessons of the Tory Health Service
1. Closing of Bart's

To-day we have closing of Bart's. Yesterday,
We had health service franchises. And to-morrow morning,
We shall have what to do after being fired. But to-day,
To-day we have closing of Bart's. Virginia
Said London did not need all these beds,
So to-day we have closing of Bart's.

These are the upper wards. And these
Are the lower wards. And this is the Op Theatre
Where the curtain is shortly to fall.
Here the sick have come for eight hundred years
And in its survival the NHS has played a part.
Yet to-day, to-day it is profit itself which is sick.

Doctors resign at the Government's decisions,
And nurses hint at strikes across the land.
The Queen herself says her bit, and Labour cries
Louder for Virginia's fall into a Bottomley pit.
No matter. The market rules all – and that is why,
To-day, to-day we must have closing of Bart's.

With apologies to HENRY REED

We'll Go No More A-Busking

So we'll go no more a-busking
So late into the night,
Though our hearts be full of singing
And our songs be still as bright.

For the station manager's unreasonable,
Says, 'The singer outwears the song',
Says, 'My staff are getting ill',
And, 'Don't hang around for long'.

Though the night was made for singing,
And the day returns too soon,
Yet we'll go more a-busking
Because L U can't recognise a good tune.

With apologies to LORD BYRON

33

from **The Wasteland**

April is the cruellest month, bringing
The tax man out of his dead office,
Ruining salaries and bonuses, drenching
Our balances with a rain of demands.

On Moorgate Station
I can connect
Nothing with nothing
For that is all that is usually left.
I have measured out my life in Tax
Returns:
This is how the world ends
Not with a bang but an overdraft.

With apologies to T. S. ELIOT

The Tube Traveller

'Is there anybody there?' said the Commuter,
Knocking on the driver's door;
And the passengers in the silence read their papers
Or stared at the carriage's dusty floor:
And some snoring drifted in from the air vent,
Above the Commuter's head:
And he hammered the door a second time;

'Are you awake in there or what?' he said.
But no one replied to the Commuter;
Least of all the driver who was practically dead.
He was dreaming of a moonlit forest
And a horse champing on deep green ferns
And a world without commuters and schedules
Bathed in moonlight at his every turn.
Then came to him a banging, soft then louder still
Until opening his eyes he started –
Well, wouldn't you, at a horse on the Bakerloo?

With apologies to WALTER DE LA MARE

Tube Sonnet

What seats my trousers have kissed, and where, and why,
I have forgotten, and what arm rests have lain
Under my elbow till Holborn; but the tunnel
Is full of ghosts tonight, that tap and sigh
Upon the glass and listen for reply.
What shall I tell them as we rattle along,
Through Bank and Chancery and Tottenham Court?
That the journey is tiresome more often than not?
That the commuter's lot is a sorry one, not worth a jot?
No, I shall tell them the rails sing with joy,
That the air is like wine and the staff deserve a clap.
Then I'll point to my head and say 'Mind the gap'.

With apologies to EDNA ST VINCENT MILLAY

Sonnet for Marcel

When to the sessions of sweet silent thought
I summon up remembrance of things past,
I wonder: Were there days when Proust got out of sorts?
When with furrowed brow he new wailed dear Time's waste,
Or, heading for the bathroom, stubbed his big toe in haste?
In truth I think there were.
Man cannot live by Madeleine cake alone
And the best of us suffer days when the tears do flow.
For these reasons to Marcel I raise a glass
And remember a Normandy farmer who
Knew him in the past:
'Marcel thought so much 'ee missed zee truth,
That's when I said, zee chickens
'Ave come 'ome to Proust'.

With apologies to SHAKESPEARE

To the Common, SW12

Glory be to God for Clapham things –
For plane-speckled skies like an M25 on high;
For brainless anglers at the pond all night;
Barboured yuppies' braying shouts; Canada geese's unholy din;

Landscape so abused and dulled – trees, grass,
Flowers amid fumes that fly;
Yet still it breathes despite car engines
Nibbling endlessly at its rim.

The draught at Clapham South – constant, cold, strange;
People who say 'Cl'm' (who knows why?);
With swift hand a Picture House appears,
He fathers forth Tea Time and the South Circular too;
Praise Him (and see you in the Windmill later).

With apologies to GERARD MANLEY HOPKINS

London Crow

Is without world

Blacker than black
Blacker even than the Northern
And that's pretty black.

Scrag end of McDonald's
Scythed with savage beak.
'Anything else, sir?'
Yes, your two clear eyes.

I am winged Hell
Cracking God's earth.
I am noon's midnight
Sending a chill to the child.

Parks are graveyards
Cemeteries my playground.
After your train has sped
I scratch the rails.

Hate me.
I laugh and mock you
Since before Time,
Caw! Caw!
I hold Creation
In my clawed foot.

Overall, the hawk in the rain
Is friendlier.

With apologies to TED HUGHES

London Leisure

What is this life if, full of care,
We have no time to stand and swear.

No time to stand on the pavements' edges
And swear as much as the wretched cabbies.

No time to yell at Oxford Street's crowds,
'Get out of the way or I'll mow you all down!'

No time to see when a courier shoots past,
His unwashed ponytail, flapping around his arse.

No time to wonder as we roll a joint,
Why it's always so windy beneath Centre Point.

No time to listen to the mad drunk's ravings,
As he opens a Tennent's and collapses on the railings.

A poor life this if, full of care,
We have no time to stand and swear.

With apologies to W. H. DAVIES

On Commuting and Mortality

Gather ye ticket stubs while ye may,
Old Time is still a-flying,
And these same passengers who smile today,
Tomorrow will be crying.
('Coz LU are all on strike, tee hee)

With apologies to ROBERT HERRICK

Retirement Blues

Stop all the clocks, cut off the telephone,
Prevent the staff from carping with a Season Ticket loan,
Silence the copiers and with little aplomb,
Bring out the glass decanter – then I'll be gone.

Let the indicator at Victoria clatter overhead
Bearing the office message 'We wish you were dead',
Put crappy bows on the neck of the coffee machine
Let the caffeine continue to make you all mean.

The Northbound, the Southbound, the East and West,
Those trains were my working week, even my Sunday rest.
The Tube was my heartbeat, my breath, my song
I thought working would last for ever: I was wrong.

My memos are not wanted now; tear up every one;
Pack up my desk and dismantle the CD Rom;
Pour away my coffee and sweep up my litter;
Let's hope in the empty days to come, I'll be not bitter.

With apologies to W. H. AUDEN and
FOUR WEDDINGS AND A FUNERAL

Other Cargoes

Sleepy staff of Debenhams from down Oxford Street
Nodding home to Croydon past sunny Thornton Heath,
With a cargo of magazines,
And tapes and stockings,
Badedas, bath soaps, and new clean sheets.

Grubby squeaking carriages coming from Victoria,
Sweeping through the 'Junction by Arding & Hobbs' flag,
With a cargo of office folk,
Booking clerks, secretaries,
Typists, and programmers, and men with bags.

Dirty Brighton coaster with pigeon-stained Buffet car
Heading towards the Downs in the sad summer eves,
With a cargo of tired dreams,
Dashed hopes, lost loves,
Regrets, desires and soft prayers breathed.

With apologies to JOHN MASEFIELD

BR's 'Fairies'

Up the airy mountain
Down the rushy glen,
We daren't go a-commuting
For fear of little men;

Stern folk, Inspector folk
Poncing on our brothers;
Black caps, gold braids,
And mean like no others!

With apologies to WILLIAM ALLINGHAM

A Red, Red Bus

O my Luve's like a red, red bus,
That's newly sprung in June;
O my Luve's like a glorious Routemaster
That sees my Requests and plays my tune.

Sometimes I'm on top, by bonnie lass,
Others ye have me below;
But I will love thee still, my Dear,
Which e'er way ye want me to go.

Wi' your curves and corners, O my sweet,
Ye have me following night and day;
Till a' the yellows gang fade in the street
I'll nae leave ye along the way.

So fare thee well on life's red route,
Let your headlights show the path;
And when your spark plugs have all run dry
They'll be a garage for ye in my heart.

With apologies to ROBBIE BURNS

Telephone Lines from Endymion

A bill from BT is a pain for ever:
Its ugliness increases; it will never
Pass into nothingness; but still will keep
Reappearing in red, ruining our quiet bower,
Haunting our dreams, making us wish we'd
Paid the bloody thing straight off instead

'BT is greed, greed BT,' – that is all
Ye know on earth, and all ye need to know.

With apologies to JOHN KEATS

NW3 Sonnet

Hampstead be not proud, though some have called thee
Haughty and disdainful, for thou art not so – thou art worse.
About McDonald's thou didst complaineth years ago
And staff in Waterstone's look down their noses at folk like me.
Yet the same air that doth blow upon your streets
Blows too across Croydon and Thornton Heath;
The same beer drunk in your pubs
Is sampled too in downmarket northern clubs.
Your chattering classes with their precious parties
Are just a bunch of arty farties.
Your beloved therapists and their bloody analysis
Aren't worth a jot in the *final* analysis
(for us it'd certainly mean financial paralysis!)
So let us leave your Blue plaqued houses and writers' blocks
One short Tube ride, we can emerge elsewhere
And Hampstead shall be no more, Hampstead thou shalt die.

With apologies to JOHN DONNE

Mind the Gyre

'Turning and turning in the widening gyre' —
The reader thinks, 'What is a gyre? Is it something
I can use, like a tyre, with which it rhymes?
Or is it something I can cash in,
Like a Giro, which I've used oft times?'
Meanings fall apart; the mind cannot hold them;
That's the trouble with English Lit.
Of words like 'gyre' one does soon tire
And as each rough syllabled beast comes round
One slouches to the dictionary
Hoping understanding shall at last be born.

With apologies to W. B. YEATS

Sonnet at Journey's End

Shall I compare thee to a ticket collector?
Thou art more lovely and more even tempered
('T would not be hard!)
Rough hands do take the darling tickets of May
And one's yearly Season hath all too short a date.
Sometimes my photocard is checked
Other times I am waved through at the gate:
This inconsistency doth leave me perplex'd
But 'tis not the traveller's place to question why,
For I know that at my journey's end –
(Despite snow that doth have some error and
Leaves that lieth where they shouldst not) –
I shall find thee waiting by our fire's grate,
And thy eternal summer shall never fade
Even though Knapp's boys often make me late.

With apologies to SHAKESPEARE

Finsbury

I will arise and go now, and go to Finsbury,
And a small ticket office build there, of clay and wattles made:
Nine self-service machines will I have there,
And a snack bar for the hungry,
And live alone and ply the commuter trade!

With apologies to W. B. YEATS

Ode to a Frightening Ale

My heart aches, and a drowsy numbness pains
My sense, as though of 'winter warmer' I had drunk
Or emptied some Tennent's Extra to my brains
One minute past, and floor-wards had sunk:
'Tis not through envy of both you fine drinks,
But being too happy in thy bubbliness,
That thou, dark or light-toned God-in-a-glass
In some tavern's kinks
Of darkened wood, and shadows numberless,
Burble like Bacchus and land folk on their arse.

With apologies to JOHN KEATS

If – (dedicated to the Northern Line)

If you can keep your place when all about you
Are losing theirs and blaming it on you,
If you can balance between stations when all men shove you
But make allowance for their shoving too;
If you can see 'Correction' on the overhead indicator
And being irritated, don't deal in irritation,
Or being late, don't give up and try to be later,
And yet don't look smug, nor walk too tall:

If you can scream – and not make screaming your master;
If you can think 'I must get out' and yet stay on;
If you can meet with Destitution and Begging
And respect each unfortunate's tattered dominion;
If you can allow the Guard his small kingdom
Behind that iron bar at the silver carriage's end
And not despair as he reads his *Sun*
And ignores his passengers, crushed on the Camden bend:

If you can take the City branch instead of the other,
And not curse the indicator which led to your mistake;
If you can walk for ever, up the stationary escalator,
And enjoy the heavy steps though your legs do so ache,
If you can wobble at Clapham as the trains pass either side
Yet keep a sweet reason as the dust flies in your face,
Or when the ticket gate says 'Seek Assistance',
Not feel like booting it all over the wretched place:

If you can tolerate crowds (for be sure you will have to),
And suffer queues on Fridays that behave like a zoo:
If neither delays nor garbled announcements hurt you,
Nor that one slow door infuriate you;
If you can fill the unforgiving minutes
With fine thoughts that (unlike the trains) run and run,
Then yours is the Earth and everything that's in it,
And – what is more – you'll make a great Guard, my son!

With apologies to RUDYARD KIPLING

Not Working but Skiving

Nobody heard him, the bored man,
But still he lay moaning:
I was much more bored than you thought
And not working but skiving.

Poor fool, he always loved doodling
And now he's dead
It must have been the copier jamming
That final time they said.

Oh, no no no, it was always jamming
(Still the dead one lay moaning)
I was far too bored all my life
And not working but skiving.

With apologies to STEVIE SMITH

The Sick Roads

O Roads thou art sick.
The invincible traffic
That rises in the morn
And soon becomes frantic,

Has found out thy beds
Of tarmacked joy:
And with unstoppable force
Does our lives destroy.

With apologies to WILLIAM BLAKE

The Passionate Spotter to his Train

Come live with me, and be my love,
And we will all my numbers move
From one end of the room to another,
Until with despair cries my mother:

'Good God! dear boy, will you never stop?
And what's that train doing in here, you clot!'
By shallow embankments shall we embrace
And plan a family, a master race!

So unbuckle your carriages, ignore the buffers
Never mind those passengers, they're just duffers.
Follow me home my many-wheeled dove,
Come live with me, and be my love.

With apologies to CHRISTOPHER MARLOWE

Daffodils

I wandered lonely as a cloud
That floats on high o'er Perivale and Hillingdon,
When all at once I saw a crowd transfixed by
A host of dancing Daffodils;
'No wonder,' thought I in the breeze,
'In Hillingdon you're lucky to see even trees.'

Continuous as the traffic that whines
And stinks along the Uxbridge Road
They stretched in never ending line
Causing many a car to be slowed.
Ten thousand I saw at a glance –
Shoppers that is, stopped in a trance.

As for the Daffs, they continued to dance –
There's little else to do in Hillingdon town:
A passing poet, could not be but gay,
Though Wordsworth would at this word now frown.
I gazed – and gazed – but little thought
What wealth this High Street show had to me brought.

For oft in Tube trains when I sit
In vacant or in pensive mood
(though usually like a comatose twit),
They flash upon the inward eye;
And then like a sparkling robe my heart doth don
The Daff-watching pillocks of Hillingdon.

With apologies to WILLIAM WORDSWORTH

Kubla Khan Takes Junction 31 off the M25

In Lakeside Thurrock did Kubla Khan
A stately shopping centre decree:
Where Ralph, the sacred porter ran,
Through aisles measureless to man
Down to a sunless check-out.
So twice five miles of fertile parking space
With walls and towers were girdled round!
Ralph one day stopped his stacking
And said to a cashier by the racking:
'Produce, produce, everywhere,
Doesn't it make you think?
Produce, produce, everywhere,
Those bananas are starting to stink.'

With apologies to SAMUEL TAYLOR COLERIDGE

Vitae Summa Brevis Spem Nos Vetat Incohare Longam*

They are too long, the weeping and the torture,
Strikes and delays and hate:
I think they have a large portion in us
After we pass the gate.

They are too long, the days of lines and roads:
Out of the tunnel's dream
Our train emerges for a while, then plunges us
Back with a scream.

* 'Let the passengers off the train first please . . .
Stand clear of the doors'.

With apologies to ERNEST DOWSON

He wishes for the Staff-room's Tea-cloths

Had I the staff-room's encrusted cloths
Saturated with tea and horribly off-white,
The brown and the thin and the torn cloths
Of shift after shift through dawn's half-light,
I would use the cloths to dry your cups;
But I, being sacked, have only my sleeves;
I have used my sleeves to dry your cups;
Drink carefully, because I didn't wash my shirt.

With apologies to W. B. YEATS

To SE16

Hail to thee, Rotherhithe spirit!
Suburb thou never wert,
That from the Thames, or near it,
Pourest across Southwark Park,
Your choking smells, disturbingly like a fart.

Gateway to your very own tunnel!
Beneath our glorious river thou sendest,
Like beetles to the dung-hill,
Traffic that never endeth
Roaring and roaring 'til it drives us round the bendeth.

Proud defender of the shortest Tube!
From Whitechapel to New Cross Gate
The East London Line is like Rubik's Cube:
No matter how many times we have to wait
We keep coming back for more and
Suspend our hate.

With apologies to PERCY BYSSHE SHELLEY

Lost Property

I shot an arrow into the air
It fell to earth, I knew not where;
Some days I simply haven't a clue,
Others I'm convinced it was Waterloo.

I left an umbrella on a carriage –
Well isn't it just as common as marriage?
Like the arrow it was straight and true,
Perhaps that too is in Waterloo.

But one day long past of rising skies,
I shall never forget – the joy, the surprise!
For there they were, wobbling together
On the Sutton train, enjoying the weather!

With apologies to HENRY WADSWORTH LONGFELLOW

Golf-Fever

I must go down to the tees again, to the lonely sixth and the
    sky,
And all I ask is a fine ball and a breeze to see her fly,
And the sun's dance and the wind's song and the green's flag
    shaking,
And a black look on my friend's face as he sees his lead
    breaking.

I must go down to the tees again, for the call of the caddy's
    trolley
Is a wild call and a clear call and one that is so jolly;
And all I ask is a sunny day with the white clouds hanging,
And the five wood and the three-iron
And a birdie for bagging.

With apologies to JOHN MASEFIELD

Commuter Doggerel

Monday's train is completely packed,
Tuesday's train is equally stacked,
Wednesday's train is oh so slow,
Thursday's train makes you want to throw,
Friday's train is subject to strikes,
Saturday's train can do what it likes,
As can the train on the Sabbath day
Because you're not on either, hip hip hurray!

(With apologies to children everywhere)

Shelley gets Hip

Rap music, when soft voices die,
Grates in the memory –
Snoop Doggy Dog, when his song is done
Lives within the headache that has now begun.

Rhymes, when the rappers are dead,
Are heaped for the DJs dishevelled bed –
And so thy thoughts, when thou art gone,
Rhythm itself shall stumble on . . .

With apologies to PERCY BYSSHE SHELLEY

Blue Remembered Seats

Into my heart an air that kills
From yon far tunnel blows:
What are those blue remembered seats,
What windows, what sliding doors are those?

That is the train of lost content
I see it shining plain,
The happy carriage where once I sat
And cannot sit again
('coz I got nicked last week for riding without a ticket).

With apologies to A. E. HOUSMAN

Mark Antony Addresses the 5.32
to Haywards Heath

'Friends, Romans, countrymen – Tickets please!
I come to book Caesar, not to praise him.
The Zone-jumping that men do amazes me;
Fare evasion must be in their bones,
Or at least so it seems with Caesar,
For just this last week or so he hath
Gone from Four to Five with a ticket for Three.'

Just then Inspector Antony turned to
Caesar's companion whose card was also raised.
'Good God!' he said. '*Et tu*, Brutus!
Don't you know that's a card for Two
And this is Five? Doest thou takest me for a ride?
You're out at Three Bridges . . . .'

With apologies to SHAKESPEARE

The Tyger

Tyger Tyger, burning bright,
In the forests of the night;
What immortal hand or eye,
Could frame thy fearful symmetry?

I'll tell you what bleedin' hand:
The same one that nabbed me in Tottenham!
For God's an Inspector of that I've no doubt,
That's why when I die, I'm giving him a clout!

With apologies to WILLIAM BLAKE

This is the Key

This is the key of the kingdom:
In that kingdom there is a station.
In that station there is an atrium.
In that atrium there is a ticket hall.
In that ticket hall there is a desk.
In that desk there is a cupboard.
In that cupboard there is a safe.
In that safe there is a box.
In that box there is a shelf.
On that shelf there is a folder.
In that folder there are some timetables.
Timetables in the folder.
Folder on the shelf.
Shelf in the box.
Safe in the cupboard.
Desk in the ticket hall.
Ticket hall in the atrium.
Atrium in the station.
Station in the kingdom.
Of the kingdom this is the key.
Now will someone please tell me when the next sodding
train to Tonbridge leaves?

With apologies to Anonymous
(whichever station he or she works in)

O Little Town of Basildon

O little town of Basildon,
How dull we think you are!
With your Essex men, Essex girls
And their white socks at the bar.
Yet in thy dark streets shineth
The everlasting light;
The one outside the takeaway –
I'll meet you there tonight.

O morning stars, together proclaim:
Another hangover!
The fourth one this week – will it end?
I doubt it, pour me another.
For shopping is driving me mad
You must now all agree;
My overdraft is out of control
Will I ever be free?

How noisily, how noisily,
The expensive gifts are bought.
So God imparts to human hearts
Credit cards and greedy thoughts.
All ears may hear their coming,
Some bargains for to find;
The poor shop staff can't stand much more,
'Jesus, this is such a bind.'

O grumpy child of Basildon,
Be happy with this gift;
The batteries have already run out
I'm really in the sh—— trouble!
We hear the Christmas angels
The great glad tidings tell:
Just three hundred and sixty-five days
Then we're back here in this hell.

With apologies to carol singers everywhere

Blake goes Shopping

And did those feet in ancient time
  Walk among Croydon's towers grey?
And was the mighty Whitgift Centre
  Built upon retail space so prime?

And did shining Allders stand so high
  It drew people from Norwood's hills?
And was Jerusalem builded here
  Among these dark Satanic tills?

Bring me my Visa (you'll see it's Gold):
  Bring me my Debenhams card too:
Bring me my cash: O notes to fold!
  Bring me those store guides to view!

I will not cease the shoppers' fight,
  Nor shall these bags rest in my hand,
Till we have built Jerusalem
On Croydon's (once) green and pleasant land.

With apologies to WILLIAM BLAKE

Ring Out, Big Ben

Ring out, Big Ben, across the fountains' hiss,
   The tourists' cries, the drunks' hullabaloo:
   The year is dying, and so are you –
For a piss, that is, and then a kiss.

Ring out the old, ring in the new,
   Wring out the washing, *that* you'll have to do:
   The Square's pigeons have done their bit –
You've started the year covered in shit.

Ring for a taxi, there's nothing quicker,
   'Streatham at 4 a.m.? That'll be fifty nicker.'
   Home at dawn with the world still spinning,
Head down the toilet – now you've stopped grinning.

That night in a dream you meet over a beer,
   The man who stands at the gate of the year;
   The old fool means well but is a bit of a jerk –
How can you tell him you just don't want to go to work?

With apologies to ALRED LORD TENNYSON

The Two-Wheeled, 17-Geared Windhover
For all city cyclists

I caught this morning morning's courier, kingdom of daylight's peddaler, roadmud-splattered torn
 T-shirt wearing warrior, in
    his riding
  of the rolling never level underneath him unsteady
    tarmac,
Pavement-hopping two-wheeled gazelle, thick-tyred stag
    locking handlebar horns against
      the West End's savagery.

Free-wheeling now, look how he skims the gutter's litter
   and pauses by the pock-marked bollard,
Then, in ecstasy!, he's off, off again to Soho or
      the City,
barking 'P O B!' to his shoulder ('Parcel on board' to
     us stationary folk trapped like flecks of shell
       in London's rotten yolk)
Like a street level falcon he rebuffs the
      big wind (last night's curry)
      scything it aside the wrong way on One Ways.
My heart in hiding stirred for a cyclist – the achieve of,
      the gall of him!

Fluorescent beauty and flickering lights
     and Lycra shorts – the whole blur not just
Derailleur but *de rigeur* too.
A billion times lovelier than oil-dappled dragon flies,
      O my courier!

To wonder at it: sheer plod makes foot folk suffocate
    in the crowd. But you shine, my dear,
and with you our spirits soar – O cyclists!
   Rise up and with gash gold-vermilion Sam Brown belts
     courier your way to paradise!

With apologies to GERARD MANLEY HOPKINS

Howl (for all street entertainers)

I saw the best mimes of my generation destroyed by
disinterest,
    starving, hysterical, knackered,
dragging themselves through Covent Garden piazza at dusk,
    looking for a hungry audience,
angelheaded jugglers burning for the ancient heavenly
                       connection
with the starry-eyed suburban maidens on the Punch & Judy
                            balcony,
    penniless thesps who stay up late in Hackney flats,
smoking weed in the supernatural darkness,
    unicyclists who scrape at heaven's belly
hoping that God or the Buddha will catch a flaming club,
    buskers who sing of the road and Dylan and Guthrie,
rough-voiced hitchhikers across the universe of music
    whose mantra is their very step on the pavement

To you all: keep the faith within your soul
    and that hat will one day overflow with coins.

With apologies to ALLEN GINSBERG

When I Survey the Wondrous 'Cross

When I survey the wondrous 'Cross,
In which our Northern trains arrive,
And see the dome rise triumphant 'bove the dross,
And side-step the junkies barely alive;

When I read the indicator's elevated poem,
Those Scottish names so redolent of heather,
Pitlochry, Aviemore – O there to roam!
Montrose, Kirkaldy – don't ask about the weather;

When I smell the diesel fumes,
Hanging as purple as the heather just mentioned,
Drifting over platforms like a cloak of doom,
Choking our arteries' every bend;

When I taste the 'customers'' snacks,
Available along the station's edges,
Coffee that's used to clean the tracks,
Bread that could double as winter sledges;

Then do I feel with a hint of surprise,
That the 'Cross is more than just a grubby palace,
It is to me the goal, the prize,
A veritable temple, London's own golden chalice.

With apologies to ISAAC WATTS

Macbeth takes the Bakerloo

Tube sorrow, and Tube sorrow, and Tube sorrow,
Hangs in this scruffy train every bloody day,
To the last syllable of recorded 'Mind the gap';
And all our yesterdays it was just the same
Back to our ancestors' death. Out, out,
Passengers' Charter! You're no use to us here.
Commuting's a worker's curse, a vile blight
That lasts for hours to our rage,
And then is heard no more ('til Monday). It is a trial
Endured by idiots, full of shoving and fury,
Signifying nothing – except . . .
Tube sorrow, and Tube sorrow, and Tube sorrow,
Hangs in this scruffy train every bloody day,
To the last syllable of recorded 'Mind the gap';
And all our yesterdays it was just the same
Back to our ancestors' deaths. Out, out,
Passengers' Charter! You're no use to us here.
Commuting's a worker's curse, a vile blight
That lasts for hours to our rage.
And then is heard no more ('til Monday). It is a trial
Endured by idiots, full of shoving and fury,
Signifying nothing – except . . .
Tube sorrow, and Tube sorrow, and *etc etc ad nauseam,*
or until the next strike.

With apologies to SHAKESPEARE

from Elegy Written in a London Suburb

The skateboard scrapes the knell of parting day,
The flowing muck winds slowly down the Lea,
The secretaries begin to wend their weary way,
And leave the world to streetlights and to me.

Now fades the graffiti by the tracks,
And all the air a solemn stillness holds,
Save for the DJs playin' garage and scratch,
And the satellite rumble of UK Gold.

Now see Blockbusters start to sell their dreams,
To teenager, yuppie and solitary saddo,
While far from the madding crowd it seems,
The dark Thames laps at each deepening shadow.

This melancholy scene is nightly repeated,
From Harrow Weald to furthest Staines,
And though the city can often leave us defeated,
Such suburban song will ease the pains.

With apologies to THOMAS GRAY

from **The Rubáiyát of Tótteridge and Whetstóne**

Awake! for Morning in the Bowl of Night
Has rung the Bell that puts the Fluffers to Flight:
   And Lo! the first Train from Barnet has brought
The Workers to the City in the gathering Light.

The Hanging Indicator writes; and, having writ,
Moves on: nor all thy Hope, nor Passion
   Shall lure it back to cancel that 'Correction',
Nor all thy Tears change your Train's direction.

To work you must go, though your Being recoils,
And this Darkness you feel will be with you Tomorrow,
   Your Cup of Life holds an oil of Sorrow –
What's more there's that Tenner you had to borrow.

Why must we hurry hither? you ask the Sky:
Whither must we hurry whence? And why?
   Hurrying hither surely heralds withering worry –
By such Seeds of Wisdom shall ye be known.

And the Universe answer'd: 'You are a Vessel
Floating o'er Time's many-hued Sea.
   In this Dance of Day and Night
It is You and You alone who decides to Happy be.'

'Yes,' you cry. 'That may be so,
But oft it seems that London's Heav'n
   Cloaks a City that seems by Madness Driv'n –
Yet declaim this in Totteridge and you'll meet Derision!'

With apologies to EDWARD FITZGERALD

80

Soliloquy on the 8.20

All the world's a train,
And all the men and women merely passengers:
They have their exits and their entrances;
And one man in his time pays many penalty fares,
His 'acts' being seven ages. At first the infant,
Mewling and puking in his mother's arms –
Too young for a ticket, surely!
And then the devious schoolboy with his Pogs and Nintendo,
'I ain't payin' a fare, no-way-do.' And then the lover
Who sighs with heart: 'I picked up these
Flowers instead of my Pass.'
Not forgetting the students who'll
Try anything for a laugh;
Or the parents who claim 'I left it in the car',
Or those early retirees who always travel too far.
And so to the last scene of all
That ends this tale of fare dodgers all:
We know them all too well –
The pensioners who give hell.
Sans teeth, *sans* eyes, *sans* taste, *sans* Rail Pass.

With apologies to SHAKESPEARE

For Network SouthEast

I sing the body electric,
These carriages that I love engirth me and I engirth them,
And with a rush we all get engirthed together.

I celebrate my journey and sing my journey
And where I commute you shall commute,
For every swishing mile belonging to me as good belongs to you.

Afoot and light-hearted (on Fridays at any rate)
I take to the iron road,
A coffee by my side (ouch! damn lids), the city before me.

Soft seats beneath me! Luggage racks above my head!
I embrace you in the dark of Three Bridges.
I am large. I contain multitudes (many of them standing).

Sussex fields below me! I see you through these windows.
You Croydon towers! You embankments! You buddleia!
You are nothing less than the journey-work of the stars.

O driver! My driver! our cheerful trip is done.
When we reach Victoria, fellow workers,
It shall come to pass – those leaves on the line
Were simply leaves of grass.

With apologies to WALT WHITMAN

'Mind the Gap' Rap (Word up! Yo!)

Mind the gap! Mind the gap!
Everybody, everybody,
Mind the gap!

You feel pretty mean,
'Coz you're on the scene,
You take the Tube
'Coz you like to be seen.
Mind the gap! Mind the gap! . . .

You travel like no other,
You're a Northern Line brother,
Tunnels comin' at ya',
You're a real commutin' mother.
Mind the gap! Mind the gap! . . .

Up town, down town,
Swing it around,
The Underground's
The funky way to get down.
Mind the gap! Mind the gap! . . .

Grandmaster Flash may take a cab.
Some of us just ain't got that cash,
Train comin' in, lookin' fab,
See the straps hangin' 'n make your grab.
Mind the gap! Mind the gap! . . .

With apologies to rappers everywhere

Aldwychcraft

Are those buildings tempting me?
Pale stones' sly sexy stare,
As if clad in underwear,
It's Aldwychcraft.

And I've got no defence for it,
That street just makes me gag for it,
What use is common sense to me here?

'Coz it's Aldwychcraft!
Wicked Aldwychcraft!
And although I know it's only a street,
When you arouse the need in me,
I see your curve surrounding me,
I want what you are leading me to.

It is such an ancient street,
And one that I'll always greet,
There ain't no nicer Aldwych than you!

'Coz it's Aldwychcraft!
Coo coo Aldwychcraft!
And although I know it's only a street,
When you arouse the need in me,
Bush House is spreading over me,
I want what you are leading me to.

It is such an ancient street,
And one that I'll always greet,
There ain't no nicer Aldwych than you!

With apologies to COLEMAN & LEIGH, and FRANK SINATRA

Tube Haiku

Moonlit night
Pearl white stars –
Not that you can
See either

Down here

This Underground

This vile route of mortals, this daily trial,
This web of suffering, this seat in the dark,
This mockery of Eden, never paradise,
This subterranea built by navvies struggling
Against London clay and the river's reach,
This unhappy breed of men, this little world,
This precious maze beneath the silver city
Which serves it like the body its veins,
Or as the rigging of some ship's soaring sails straining
Against storm or heavy sea,
This blessed grubbiness, this clammy air,
This broken escalator, this poor, battered, blamed,
Blighted, bewildered and underfunded transport system,
For which, against our better judgement,
We yet feel a curious affection,
This rattling symphony, this urban mantra,
This very breath of our lives,
This Underground.

With apologies to SHAKESPEARE and *RICHARD II*

Sonnet to Victoria

How do I love thee? Let me count the ways.
I love thee to the depth and breadth and height
Of your girdered roof (look out for the pigeo—— too late)
And for *Le Croissant* shop at which les commuters,
Pigeon-like, love to graze.
I love thee from the balcony cradling Smiths
Where the brightly lit windows attract my gaze
And shine like Liberty's outstretched beacon on high
(I've been drinking next door is what you're thinking,
Boozing not browsing – that'll be another train missed).
I love the human tide that diagonally sweeps
Across your shiny floor to the Tube half-asleep
And oft times I wonder of whom they dream
As they shuffle like zombies amid the stream.
I love the tannoy's inadvertent jokes above the roar –
'Platform Seventeen for Amberly, Goring, Hastings and/Orr'.
I love thee freely, wishing nothing in return
(Well, perhaps a seat)
I love thee as purely as your shining rails
I love thee as if you were a bride in veils.

Dear reader, can you see why Victoria has my vote –
Now I promise to go quietly with the men in white coats.

With apologies to ELIZABETH BARRETT BROWNING

Desiderata Revisited

'Go mental amid the noise and haste – no one's going to blame you, it's a madhouse down there – and remember what peace there may be with a Kalashnikov. As far as possible be on good terms with all persons, particularly Inspectors, for they too have their story (never as unbelievable as yours). Avoid loud and aggressive passengers, they are vexatious to the spirit. If you compare yourself with First Class travellers you may become vain and bitter; for always there will be greater and lesser persons than yourself – these are the ones to push in front of on the escalator. Enjoy your achievements as well as your plans, however pathetic you worthless piece of scum. Exercise caution when travelling out of Zone; for the world is growing wise to your trickery. But let this not blind you to what opportunities exist; many officials are too dozy to look at your ticket properly. Be yourself. Do not feign executive status when you have none. Neither be cynical about others' promotions; for you can always smirk and just wipe their hard disk when they're at lunch. Take kindly what isn't yours, gracefully slipping into your pocket anything you can. Nurture strength of spirit to shield you in sudden misfortune, particularly if you travel on the Northern. But do not distress yourself with imaginings – those are mice, not rats, down there amongst the McDonald's wrappers. Beyond a wholesome discipline (except over your finances which are a hopeless case) be gentle with yourself. You are a child of the universe no less than the trees and the stars; you have a right to be here. Unfortunately you are also a child of Network SouthEast, but try not to think about it. And whether it is clear to you, no doubt the universe is unfolding as it should – with more and more roads and poorer and poorer air. Therefore be at peace with God, even though He doesn't commute. And whatever your labours and aspirations to get a seat, in the noisy confusion of the Tube keep peace with your soul. With all its muck, drudgery and incomprehensible announcements, it still gets you to work. What else are you going to do? Walk? Be cheerful. Strive to be happy. That is, Strap-happy.'

With apologies to MAX EHRMANN, and LES CRANE,
who got to number one with this in 1972

INDEX OF FIRST LINES